PRAYER IS MY WEAPON & *I'm Loaded*

LEARNING HOW TO APPLY THE PRINCIPLES OF GOD

Joyce Goudy

© Bringing your words to life

Copyright © 2025 by Trinity Publishing Company

All rights reserved. No part of this book may be reproduced or transmitted in any form or by any means, electronic or mechanical, including photocopying, recording, or by any information storage and retrieval system, without permission in writing from the author, except for the inclusion of brief quotations in a review.

Published in USA by Trinity Publishing Company

Paperback ISBN: 978-1-964707-54-9

Book Cover: R. Muhammad

Formatting: Paul Nomshan

GREETINGS, WARRIOR,

I speak and believe by faith that whoever reads this book is part of the remnant Isaiah speaks of in chapter 69—a chosen people of God for a set time. You are a remnant that has endured much fire yet refuses to die in transition. You are a true warrior and part of a royal priesthood.

Here is a little background on why I am so passionate about teaching others how to live a lifestyle of prayer. Prayer has taken me on a journey, and over time, I have experienced tremendous growth that does not come from man. God placed this book in my heart to write for those seeking to understand how to grow in prayer. There were many times I found myself in long seasons of frustration—praying for change yet seeing no results for years. I later discovered that my lifestyle and mindset had to align with what I was praying for. It wasn't until I began releasing certain people, places, and things that I noticed God drawing nearer to me with His presence in its fullness.

I learned the hard way—often without physical help from others. Yet, God Himself used my obedience and sacrifice to His word to teach me His ways. Your pain and trials can literally teach you how to pray.

These two principles—Obedience and Sacrifice—are what I call God's love language, and they will undoubtedly capture heaven's attention.

Have you ever felt like God is ignoring you or that something is missing in your prayer life? If so, this book is for you. It is filled with wisdom gained from my personal failures and growing pains with God. There were many years of suffering as I tried to learn how to pray effectively. I was frustrated when nothing seemed to change. If you love God but have been frustrated with the waiting process or feel like He is not listening to your prayers, this book is for you.

Understanding what it means to suffer in God's will from the start can help a believer embrace trials and tribulations with joy. When we understand the cost every believer must pay to follow Christ, we gain an advantage that allows us to grow even under intense pressure—especially when we realize that the anointing comes with levels of suffering.

After many nights of suffering, tears, and pain, I realized God was building my relationship with Him. He was developing within me a capacity and stamina that no one else could provide, nor could it be bought with money.

Your suffering can also be used for others, just as Jesus demonstrated. The Bible says, Isaiah 53:5 kjv

"By His stripes, we are healed." Likewise, it is through the word of our testimony that others can be healed. This book is my testimony of how the Word of God works when applied with understanding, helping you to live a lifestyle of worship.

Prayer is work, so don't be too hard on yourself. This walk of Holiness is no joke, it will break you down & build you back up. Consider this to be a fresh start and a new journey. Prayer reflects your relationship with the Father, and developing a strong prayer life takes time. Clean hands and a pure heart that please God—not man—are essential.

Prayer gives you access to the Father in heaven! I know your life is about to change as you read and gain an understanding of His Kingdom. When you seek God first and His righteousness, everything else will be added to you. Prayer connects you to God, but how you live will keep you connected. If you're reading this book, I know you have prayed for help or wondered, *"Am I praying the right way?"* or *"How can I grow in my prayer life?"* Either way, I am proud of you in the Lord.

I write this to you by faith.

Your prayer life will never be the same after reading this book, in Jesus' name!

Welcome, Prayer Warrior! Let's get you ready to dive into this transformational journey. Here are a few simple steps to help you maximize your experience with this book.

The ministry of Pastor Joyce Goudy offers hands-on intercession training classes where you can learn to strengthen your relationship with God and connect with other prayer warriors. For more information, email **PBIPMinistry@yahoo.com**.

Get the workbook.

If you haven't already purchased the workbook, Prayer Is My Weapon & I'm Loaded—Daily Prayer Principles by Joyce Goudy, don't wait— grab it now! Whether you run, jump, hop, or simply click, make sure you have the workbook in hand, as this book is designed to work in conjunction with it. The workbook is available on Amazon, so order your copy today!

Contents

Chapter 1: Preparation for Fasting 9

Chapter 2: Making Hard Decisions. 21

Chapter 3: After Fasting, Now What?. 29

Chapter 4: I Shut the Door, but I Left the Window Open 35

Chapter 5: Peer Pressure. 39

Chapter 6: I'm Married but I Feel Single 47

Chapter 7: Hindered Prayers 53

Chapter 8: Waiting on God or Do I Move Forward? 57

Chapter 9: Living with the Inner Enemy 63

Chapter 10: The Benefits of Waiting Patiently. 67

Chapter 11: Misplaced Love/The Seed of Rejection 71

Chapter 12: I Need Help but I Don't Want Help. 75

Chapter 13: Encouraging Words. 79

Personal Prayer to Read Aloud

Dear Heavenly Father, my Lord and Savior, I come before You with humility, true hunger, and a thirst to know You and to be more like You in every area of my life. Anything in my heart or in my life that is not pleasing to You, I ask that You remove it completely so healing and deliverance can be my portion. As I read this book, Father, I ask that You set me free from all strongholds or any hidden addictions that may be covered by learned behaviors or excuses from past trauma and pain. Purify me, Lord, through the power of the Holy Ghost, in the name of Jesus Christ. I repent and ask for forgiveness for all my sins, known and unknown, in the mighty name of Jesus.

Let the breath of God breathe on the words of this book and draw me closer to You. Lord, I give You full access to my heart, mind, soul, and spirit to wash me from all impurities. Father, I pray that You will open my eyes to understand with clarity so I can see what You see, love how You love, and hate what You hate. Lord, I thank You in advance for Your love and kindness toward me, in Jesus' name. Amen.

Chapter One

Preparation for Fasting

The Challenge of Fasting

Fasting can be very challenging, especially if you haven't done it in a while. Every time you fast, there should be a level of preparation and strategic planning beforehand. Fasting unto the Lord automatically enlists you in a battleground against your flesh and the devil. Just as a U.S. soldier wouldn't go to the battlefield without armor or a strategic plan, the same applies to spiritual warfare for a child of God. Fasting elevates you into a deeper level of battle in almost every area of your life.

Purpose of Fasting

Fasting is not merely something we do to get God's attention; rather, it is a means of seeking His wisdom and divine purpose. Through worship, we draw His attention and receive the answers we need. On this journey, we uncover His original intent, seeing Him as the Creator of all things. By understanding His will, we align ourselves with His divine plan. Embracing a lifestyle of fasting ultimately leads us back to God's original foundation.

Sanctification Through Fasting

As children of God, we should fast regularly for sanctification, asking the Lord to search our hearts and purify us with His holy Word and love. Entering a fast unprepared or without understanding the true nature of the enemy can leave you feeling confused or disappointed during and even after the fast.

Identifying the True Enemy

Before you start a fast, you must identify the enemy that poses a threat or feels like an attack. For example, it may seem as if your own flesh is the enemy, but in reality, it could be the Word of God pruning you to produce more fruit. Yes, I said the Word of God—because often, it is not the devil testing you; rather, it is the Word of God being proven in your everyday life. God did this very thing to Joseph, as stated in Psalm 105:17-19. The Word of God must be tried in you through daily tribulations and decisions.

Trials and Faith in Christ

As a child of God, trials will come from every direction, ultimately leading you to rely on **Jesus Christ—our Savior, the Anointed One.** *He gave His life so that we might live through Him by faith. Just as Jesus, the Son of God, endured suffering, you too will face hardships. Yet, this suffering becomes the pathway to dying to self—the flesh—granting you access to God's abundant grace. This is the essence of His promise: You can do all things through Christ Jesus by faith. Our suffering is not in vain; it is an invitation for God to work all things together for our good.*

The Battle of Hunger

Fasting alone is difficult; abstaining from food is a battle in itself. Hunger can feel like an attack on your mind. If you're anything like me, when I'm hungry, my stomach develops a strong personality that changes my entire attitude. Words can come out of my mouth on behalf of my stomach. I have said things like, "Please just leave me alone"—in my Jackie Hill Perry voice—or "Don't bother me." In other words, fasting eventually starves the flesh, and being hungry for hours can affect your emotions and reveal undeveloped character flaws. When your stomach begins to feel empty, and irritation rises because someone is picking on you, frustration can easily lead to conflict—either with another person or within yourself.

Listen, Linda, listen—being hungry can transform you into another person. Have you ever been hungry for an extended period? It can feel like people are intentionally irritating and bothering you. Sometimes, it even seems like the world has made an announcement: "Hey, everybody! Look at them! They're fasting. Offer them free food. Say crazy stuff to them. Make them upset."

The devil is petty. He will even bring up past relationships, and suddenly, old flames will pop up on Facebook, triggering memories of sinful things that once seemed fun. A real battle begins in your mind, and at times, you can even feel temptations in your body.

Preparing for a Fast: Using Wisdom

Preparation before fasting is about using wisdom. It's not mandatory, but it can help you fight more effectively—physically and spiritually. One way to prepare is by asking the Lord to search your heart and willingly surrender any past or current situations that have caused you anger, pain, or offense. The goal is to allow God to examine your motives and uncover any unresolved hurts that may be influencing you.

As children of God, we sometimes do things that seem right but are driven by wounded motives. Jeremiah 17:9 reminds us that the heart is deceitful above all things. It is possible to fast with the belief that our works will move God simply because we are hurting. A deceitful heart can even lead us to manipulate scripture to justify our actions, rather than seeking God's truth.

The Power of Understanding Scripture

Satan is not intimidated by our knowledge of scripture. He only flees when we understand how to use God's Word and apply it in our lives. Jesus demonstrated this in Matthew 4 when He resisted the devil's temptations during His 40-day fast by, using the correct scriptures with understanding.

As believers, we must understand that God is our Provider, Protector, and Disciplinarian. Being a child of God is more than just a declaration—it is a journey of complete dependence on Him. Many people grow up in the church, engaging in spiritual practices like fasting without fully understanding their purpose. When asked why they are fasting, they often respond, "Because the church is on a fast." However, true fasting requires revelation from the Holy Spirit, not just learned behaviors.

Examining Our Motives for Fasting

Many believers never fully grasp the true source of salvation or the depth of God's love. As a result, they engage in fasting and other spiritual disciplines without clear understanding. Without the Holy Spirit's guidance, we are left interpreting scripture through our own lens, missing its transformative power.

Sometimes, we fast only when we feel something is wrong. However, Jeremiah 17:9 warns us that our hearts are deceitful, meaning we cannot base spiritual decisions solely on our emotions. Instead, we must approach fasting with intentionality and clarity.

Making Things Right Before Fasting

It is wise to reconcile with others before starting a fast. You may even need to seek wise counsel on how to approach certain situations. The Bible provides instructions on identifying and addressing sin in our hearts, ensuring that our fasting is a sweet-smelling sacrifice to God.

Matthew 5:23-24 instructs us to reconcile with our brethren before bringing our offering to God. Genesis 4:4 further illustrates how Abel's sincere offering was accepted while Cain's was rejected. This shows that our motives, heart posture, and attitude matter to God. He desires that we give and fast with sincerity, not just out of obligation.

Defining the Enemy and Seeking Results

Once you identify the real enemy, the next step is to determine what results are you seeking from your fast. This is a conversation worth having before you begin. No one wants to fast repeatedly without seeing results—it would eventually lead to discouragement. Every fast, when done according to God's principles, should yield an outcome. There will always be a time of sowing and reaping. It is wise to ask a pastor or spiritual mentor, "What results should I be looking for in a sanctification fast?"

Fasting as Spiritual Warfare

Fasting is a battlefield, requiring every believer to wear the full armor of God. Ephesians 6 emphasizes the necessity of preparation before engaging in spiritual warfare. Paul describes in Ephesians chapters 4 and 5 how we should live in the natural before putting on spiritual armor in chapter 6.

Think about it: what good is it to wear only part of your armor? To stand firm in fasting, we must ensure we are fully equipped with the armor of God, prepared both spiritually and emotionally for the battle ahead.

The Open Door to the Enemy

All the devil needs is one open door to cause havoc in multiple areas of your life. Often, we keep people at a distance to feel secure, yet we fail to realize that spiritual protection is more important than physical security. The devil is always seeking whom he may devour. He will target any area of your life where there are unresolved matters of the heart, using fiery darts to weaken your faith and cause spiritual instability.

Identifying the Real Enemy

One of the most difficult aspects of fasting is discerning the true source of opposition. Is it your flesh, the consequences of past decisions, or the devil himself? In spiritual warfare, we seek God to fight for us both in the spiritual and natural realms. How can we ensure this? **Through our Mediator and Redeemer—Jesus Christ.** Recognizing that Jesus intercedes for us changes everything. We are not alone in this battle. Our role is to remain steadfast physically, emotionally, and spiritually, trusting that as we walk by faith, God will fulfill His role as our defender. If we find ourselves fighting against people rather than the true enemy, it is possible that the devil is manipulating us against ourselves. Unforgiveness can keep spiritual wounds open, making us vulnerable to further attacks.

Positioning Yourself in God During Fasting

When fasting, ensuring that you are in right standing with God is key. Having your heart aligned with both God and others allows you to **remain seated in heavenly places.** When God looks at you, He sees His Son, Jesus Christ. This does not mean that every situation will result in peace, but through God's power, you can love others—including your enemies—just as Christ loves you. Submitting fully to God and His Word grants Him **supreme authority** to move and demonstrate His power in every area of your life.

The Importance of a Righteous Heart in Battle

If you enter a spiritual battle with unresolved issues in your heart, it may feel like God is allowing the enemy to prevail against you rather than fighting for you. This truth may be difficult to accept, but it is necessary for victory. Understanding your position in spiritual warfare equips you to remain fully armed with the Word of God and use it effectively in prayer.

Forgiveness: A Necessary Step Before Fasting

Take a deep breath and think about those who have hurt you. Now say out loud, "Thank you, Father." This may seem strange, but 1 Timothy 3:16 reminds us of the mystery of godliness. Even as you read this, salvation and deliverance are being released over your life and family in Jesus' name.

Physical Preparation for Fasting

Forgiveness is not only a spiritual act but can also be expressed practically. While many find it easier to ask God for forgiveness in private, facing those who have wronged us can be more difficult. Sometimes, approaching someone is necessary, even if the offense was a misunderstanding or a matter of personal perception. However, wisdom is crucial, especially in situations involving legal matters or potential conflict. (think you might swing on someone) Seeking counsel can help ensure that reconciliation is approached safely and wisely.

When preparing for fasting, be open to God revealing unresolved relationships. He may bring people into your path or remind you of past events that require closure. Sometimes, He will prompt you to take action, even when the other person was at fault. This is not about weakness but about obedience and spiritual strength. As you prepare, affirm your faith boldly: "I ain't no punk in these Holy Ghost streets!"

Caring for Your Physical Health During Fasting

Fasting is both a spiritual and physical discipline. Neglecting your physical well-being can leave you vulnerable to attacks. Lack of rest, exhaustion, and poor nutrition can weaken your body and mind, making it easier for the enemy to exploit your weaknesses. Many of us, especially those with driven personalities, struggle to prioritize rest and nourishment. However, failing to do so can undermine the effectiveness of our fast.

The Connection Between Health and Spiritual Warfare

Taking care of your physical health is essential when preparing for a spiritual battle. Fasting invites spiritual warfare, and this battle can manifest in various ways—whether through cravings, workplace challenges, or internal struggles with self-discipline. **Living a lifestyle of regular fasting increases our awareness of the areas in which God is working within us.** If poor health is the result of a lack of self-control, unhealthy habits, or neglect, it can make you an easy target for the enemy during your fast.

Many times, we blame the devil for our struggles, but in reality, some of the weapons he uses against us are the very ones we have handed over through our choices. The enemy's goal remains the same: to steal, kill, and destroy. Recognizing and addressing our vulnerabilities, both spiritually and physically, empowers us to stand firm in battle and experience victory in Christ.

One way to prepare practically for fasting is by focusing on your health. Often, we start a fast emotionally but are not physically prepared. Simple things like not getting enough rest or proper nutrition can leave us vulnerable to spiritual attacks. If your body is weak, your mind becomes an easy battleground for the enemy. Prioritize rest, nourishment, and hydration as part of your fasting routine.

Studies show that a strong immune system can prevent sickness. White blood cells and proteins in a healthy body fight and eliminate disease-causing microorganisms and toxins before they cause severe illness. This aligns with God's desire for us to have self-discipline in all areas of life, including health. Taking vitamins, drinking water, and getting enough sleep are practical ways to ensure your body remains strong during a fast. As believers, we can sometimes be "so spiritual" that we neglect our physical health. However, God has given us practical tools such as regular exercise, doctor visits, and proper nutrition to maintain our well-being.

Final Thoughts

As you prepare for fasting, remember that spiritual warfare requires both spiritual and practical readiness. Align your heart with God, seek reconciliation where needed, and take care of your physical health. Through these steps, you will be fully equipped to stand strong in battle, knowing that the Lord is fighting for you. Amen.

One of the most important ways to prepare physically before fasting is by identifying the root cause of any illness rather than attributing it solely to the devil. Understanding the source of your struggles allows you to use prayer as a precise and powerful weapon. Call out the issue by name and destroy it completely from the inside out.

Key Steps to Preparation:

1. Recognize the True Enemy – Understand that not every struggle is purely physical or purely spiritual.

2. Acknowledge Past and Present Offenses – No matter how big or small, unresolved offenses can hinder spiritual growth.

3. Gain Understanding of Spiritual Armor – Study Ephesians 5-6 to discern what true spiritual armor entails.

4. Seek Biblical Wisdom – Before beginning your fast, understand the spiritual outcomes you should anticipate.

Chapter Two

Making Hard Decisions

Principle Scriptures

"But when you ask, you must believe and not doubt, because the one who doubts is like a wave of the sea, blown and tossed by the wind." – James 1:6 (NIV)

"For our struggle is not against flesh and blood, but against the rulers, against the authorities, against the powers of this dark world and against the spiritual forces of evil in the heavenly realms." – Ephesians 6:12

"And remember, when you are being tempted, do not say, 'God is tempting me.' God is never tempted to do wrong, and he never tempts anyone. Temptation comes from your own desires, which entice us and drag us away." – James 1:13-14 (NIV)

The Battle of Decision-Making While Fasting

Making decisions while fasting presents a unique form of mental and spiritual warfare. As hunger intensifies, emotions may fluctuate, and clarity may waver. Whether your fast is to draw closer to God or seek divine guidance, the enemy will attempt to attack your mind. Your thoughts become a battleground, and **staying focused on Jesus is essential for maintaining peace.**

Ask yourself: Do you have peace that comes from your relationship with Christ?

Decision-making can be particularly difficult when it involves major life changes or responsibilities that shape your destiny. At times, God may grant you a vision, yet the season you're in requires unwavering faith. The transition between divine instruction and earthly action can bring intense mental warfare. Without daily immersion in God's presence, one can fall into frustration or even depression.

True prayer is a journey that takes time, and at times, it may challenge your patience with God. Yet, gaining the knowledge of God provides spiritual weapons. Knowing your enemy and how to defeat them—both physically and spiritually—is half the battle.

Staying Focused in Spiritual Warfare

A key principle in making decisions is to remain focused on your role in the fight. As a child of God, it is crucial to understand your position in the spiritual battle. **Gaining practical wisdom may require seeking Godly counsel, fasting, praying, and waiting on divine instruction.** There will also be moments of silence from God—times when He is elevating you to higher faith and obedience, much like Abram's test with his son. Regardless of the circumstances, decision-making will always engage the mind, body, and spirit in warfare. Therefore, before entering this battle, equip yourself spiritually.

Two Fundamental Keys for Every Spiritual Warrior:

1. Assurance – Be confident in God's promises and your identity in Christ.
2. Affirmation – Declare victory in Christ before the battle even begins.

Yes, you read that right. You can celebrate now because victory is already secured through Jesus Christ! While decision-making is never easy, choosing to worship during the battle will strengthen your faith. Sometimes, even small daily decisions—like what to cook for dinner or which job to take—can cause undue stress. However, when you intentionally remind yourself of who God is, you will create a space of peace in your mind.

The Enemy's Tactic: Attacking Your Identity

One of the enemy's favorite strategies is to make you doubt your identity in Christ. For example, in Matthew 4:6-9, when Jesus was led into the wilderness, Satan did more than question Him—he attempted to cast doubt on His identity by saying, *"If you are the Son of God..."*

Likewise, when we seek guidance, the real conflict is often not about whether God is good or whether He will bless us. Instead, we struggle to believe His Word over the lies of the enemy. Faith is easier said than done, especially when tested.

To build confidence in who you are, immerse yourself in Scripture. The more you understand about your Creator, the clearer your purpose will become.

Engaging with Scripture for Guidance

Warrior, practice turning to the Bible for real-life examples that relate to your situation. The Bible is filled with testimonies that provide insight into how we can partner with God beyond mere religious routines. Prayer is powerful, but sometimes, the answers we seek require active obedience.

The Power of Obedience

Many of our victories come when we say *yes* to God—not just with our words, but with our actions. Throughout the Bible in the book of Deuteronomy, God's promises are often conditional, introduced by the word "if." When we follow His commands and acknowledge Him in all our ways, He faithfully directs our paths.

Assurance Before the Battle

Now, let's go even deeper. Understanding your position in prayer will empower you to make practical decisions based on God's truth. Knowing that Jesus has already secured your victory enables you to cast down any thought that contradicts His Word. When you enter prayer with assurance, it changes everything. And warrior, knowing that Jesus Christ has your back? That means everything!

It's like a group of people unexpectedly comes to your father's house, ready to jump you. (A street fight of five people against one) But inside, your family has your back. You know they're skilled in different weapons, trained by God Himself on how to fight. (Side note: Ain't nothing like having a family member who doesn't mind throwing hands—just kidding!)

The Holy Ghost is just that—a trained warrior with a mission: to teach you how to war in the spirit, not against the flesh. Just like in a physical battle, it's crucial to understand that heaven is backing you up. A host of angels is at your disposal to fulfill the demands of God's Word that you live. Your angelic helpers are diligently attending to God's business concerning His Son, who resides within your temple—your body.

God Stands on Business When It Comes to His Son

Zechariah 4:6 reminds us that we win battles not by our own **strength, power, or might, but by His Spirit**. It's essential to acknowledge daily that the Lord God and Savior is on your side. Within that space, your faith will grow.

Can I be honest? This may seem simple to some people. I've heard others say, "Just pray, make a decision, and move forward." However, there can be a war going on in the mind. You may have spent your entire life doing whatever you wanted, but over time, you learn to yield daily to God and the Holy Spirit. Sometimes, you may struggle to discern when something is all on you versus when you need His power to move. This is real—many believers over-spiritualize everything, and that's why so many feel stuck, saying, "I'm waiting on God."

A great woman of God named Dr. Graham once told me: *Don't be so spiritually bound that you're no earthly good.* Some people get stuck at wanting to acknowledge God (Proverbs 3:6) because they don't fully understand who He is, His role on earth, or when to walk by faith versus applying faith through works. Making decisions can be a war. Some are easy, like what to wear on your birthday or what foods you don't like. But gaining wisdom and knowledge about Jesus Christ is a weapon. Knowing your identity in Him is also a weapon. It strengthens you against the enemy's tricks and mental attacks when making hard choices. **Doubt breeds confusion**, which ultimately kills hope and faith in what God has spoken over your life.

Spiritual Warfare: Exposing Unwanted Guests

Picture this: there are unwanted guests in your house (your temple), but you can't see them unless the light is off. For my people in the back, I'm talking about those big, disrespectful water bugs and hood roaches that get hit with a newspaper, act like they're dead, then speed off to another corner. (I'm laughing as I type this, but hear me out!)

Spiritual warfare can feel just like that. Every believer should feel this way about their personal temple, where the Holy Spirit—the King—resides. Before Jesus died for our sins, He told His disciples that the Comforter, the Holy Spirit, would come after Him and that He needs a temple—*your body and mind.* Once you invite the Light of the world inside your heart, His Word will expose all uninvited guests that lurk in dark corners of your heart. Many times, we don't notice things until His light shines from within. God's Word does just that: under a bright light, hidden things begin to come out.

No Shame or Condemnation—Just Growth

Don't allow what you discover about yourself to place you in shame or condemnation, even if it takes years to realize your mistakes. God knows how to use everything for your good. Your trials and tribulations can actually draw you closer to God—if you accept His grace daily and move forward instead of allowing **guilt to breed depression**. Acknowledge your sins, repent, and keep going. Nobody is perfect, but we can be perfected through Christ Jesus.

When Trauma Hinders Your Faith

There are times when people feel defeated in prayer because life has thrown too much at them. Trauma can easily hinder the application of God's Word, especially when making tough decisions, instead of the word planting seeds of faith, here comes doubt and fear.

Let's Pray! Read this out loud.

Today, the Lord, my Father, has given me a helper—the Holy Spirit. He is my Comforter, my Teacher, and my Counselor. He will guide me in the ways of the Lord and intercede for me when I cannot find the words to pray. He will lead and guide me as I make decisions too big for me. By faith, in the name of Jesus Christ, I rebuke every spirit of doubt and fear that rises when I make decisions. I command them to leave me completely, in Jesus Christ's name. Amen.

> **Key Takeaways:**
> 1. Create a space of peace by keeping your mind on Him.
> 2. Understand your role in the battle—stay seated in heavenly places.
> 3. Have confidence in knowing who has your back.
> 4. Know when to combine faith with works—take action.
> 5. Unwanted guests are not your fault—acknowledge, repent, and move forward.

Chapter Three

After Fasting, Now What?

Principal Scriptures

"You did not choose me, but I chose you and appointed you so that you might go and bear fruit—fruit that will last—and so that whatever you ask in my name the Father will give you."
–John 15:16 (NIV)

"But seek ye first the kingdom of God, and his righteousness; and all these things shall be added unto you." – Matthew 6:33 (KJV)

Understanding the Purpose of Fasting

Fasting is not for the faint-hearted. Going without food for any length of time weakens the body, and let's be honest—who enjoys being hungry? No one. Even animals instinctively scavenge for food when they go without for too long.

Jesus references fasting about 70 times in the KJV Bible. Many believers would find fasting beneficial if they fully understood the process and had clear guidance on what to do before, during, and after.

This chapter is particularly close to my heart because it reveals how God has provided strategies through His Word to help us bear lasting fruit. I believe it is the Lord's will not only for us to live prosperous lives but also to bring forth spiritual fruit that remains.

According to John 15:16, God has chosen and ordained you to go and bear fruit that will last. The Holy Spirit within you is like a seed of truth. When you remain connected to the Vine—Christ—you will naturally bear fruit. **This is key: to see spiritual fruit after fasting, you must stay connected to the Father and nurture His Word within you.**

Just as a seed needs water to grow, the Word of God must be watered in your spirit. The Holy Spirit empowers you to overcome temptation and resist the enemy's schemes. He will convict you before you eat that piece of chicken while fasting and will teach you how to battle depression using the Word as your weapon.

Maintaining Hunger for the Kingdom

One of the biggest struggles after fasting is **maintaining a consistent hunger for the kingdom of God and His righteousness**. Too often, we return to our normal routines, attending church once or twice a week, but our spiritual discipline fades.

The Father despises lukewarmness. So, how do we combat spiritual stagnation, **especially when hurt and internal suffering creates strongholds of depression and rebellion against the Lord?**

Internal suffering can unknowingly lead us into disobedience simply due to feelings of hopelessness or exhaustion. The devil preys on these dry places in our minds and hearts. According to Luke 11:24, certain spirits try to return to their former dwelling places, whispering lies such as: "There's no purpose in repenting," or "You must not be doing something right because nothing has changed."

The enemy distorts our perception, using circumstances and distractions to discourage us. Many believers become unknowingly angry with God because they don't understand the principle of seedtime and harvest. Doubt creeps in when we don't see immediate results, leading to a loss of faith.

Understand this: you can physically attend church but still not be part of the Body of Christ. Lukewarmness manifests in various ways. We cannot afford to be around but not connected. Read that again.

Recognizing the Fruit After Fasting

Fruit originates from within. Don't be discouraged if you don't see immediate changes after fasting. Some seeds take longer to sprout. Often, we look for outward blessings—new jobs, houses, or financial breakthroughs—when in reality, true fruit is spiritual that will later show in the natural. When we focus only on material gain, we limit ourselves from receiving the Holy Spirit's transformative work.

According to Galatians 5, the fruit of the Spirit includes:
- Love
- Joy
- Peace
- Patience
- Kindness
- Goodness
- Faithfulness
- Gentleness
- Self-control

As we seek God first (Matthew 6:33), everything else will be added to us. Our primary pursuit should always be spiritual growth.

The Waiting Season

Let's be honest waiting can feel exhausting. It's easy to grow weary when we don't see progress. But don't underestimate the power of the waiting season. Just as life teaches a child wisdom through experience, your waiting season is developing you in ways that only time can produce.

Many of us give up after waiting two months, six months, a year, or three years simply because we don't see fruit. But ask yourself—did you clearly define the fruit you were looking for before the fast? The heart often hides things from us, and fasting exposes areas that need refining.

Rejection and depression don't disappear instantly just because you got baptized or completed a fast. The Bible warns us that "The heart is deceitful above all things" (Jeremiah 17:9). Some struggles only become visible under pressure. If you are in a long waiting season, take heart—God may be planting and watering something within you, preparing you for a harvest that is yet to come.

Fruit is Produced for Others

Read this slowly: fruit is produced for others to eat.

After fasting, you should be able to identify areas in your life that need growth and refinement. The Holy Spirit will reveal to you what needs development, and it is your responsibility to nurture those areas. Your relationship with Christ is a daily walk, and the Holy Spirit is ready to guide you every step of the way.

Key Takeaways:

1. Define what type of fruit you are looking for.
2. Ask yourself: Is the fruit remaining? (John 15:16)
3. Remember, some things take time to grow.
4. Fruit is a seed—it grows in seasons and requires time.
5. Fasting reveals areas that need watering (spiritual maintenance).

Let's Pray! Read this out loud.

Father, it's me again.

Lord, I ask You to hold my hand through this journey of growing and planting seeds. May the fruit of Your Son be evident in my life. Your Word says we will know who belongs to You by their fruit. Teach me Your ways and help me live out what You are teaching me.

Lord, help me not to be so hard on myself when I fall short. Break off any shame, guilt, or discouragement hidden in my heart. Do a new thing within me so that, when my harvest season comes, I will reap good fruit. In the mighty name of Jesus, Amen.

Chapter Four

I Shut the Door, but I Left the Window Open

Foundational Scriptures

"Settle matters quickly with your adversary who is taking you to court. Do it while you are still together on the way, or your adversary may hand you over to the officer, and you may be thrown into prison." — Matthew 5:25

"For we wrestle not against flesh and blood, but against the principalities, against the powers, against the world-rulers of this darkness, against the spiritual hosts of wickedness in the heavenly places." — Ephesians 6.12

Sometimes, you truly need a fresh start—a new beginning—and must be very intentional and aggressive about starting over. The Bible mentions this concept numerous times. One example is when God chose Noah and his family. Only eight people were permitted to enter the next season of "new." He instructed them to build, leave, and start over.

Many times, we disconnect from people and places but fail to shut all access points that the enemy may use spiritually later on in life to hinder our healing process. If you shut someone out of your life, it's because you've decided within yourself that you don't want any connection with them. Yet, if you've only handled the matter privately and not publicly, the door is not completely shut. This approach may work for the world, but not for believers. We live by principles of honor. If you shut the door on someone spiritually but leave the window wide open in the natural, they still have access to you.

What happens if you change your phone number but then run into that person in public? If you never expressed your feelings or closure, they remain unaware of your true stance. Though time has passed, closure was never established. **Any unresolved issue that creates confusion or distance between you and God is an opportunity for the enemy to plant a seed of offense or water a seed of rejection.**

It is your choice to disengage from relationships, but as a child of God, the Lord teaches us to honor all people—even when we choose not to befriend them. Leaving a window open causes unnecessary mental warfare because the matter was not handled promptly.

According to Matthew 12:43–45, the enemy not only seeks territory but also looks for ways to accuse us in the courts of heaven. He uses biblical principles that, if unaddressed, give him legal rights to imprison us spiritually. Yes, a believer—born again and saved—can still find themselves in spiritual bondage if they are not aligned with God's Word. In the natural, a prosecutor ensures justice by presenting evidence. Similarly, in the spiritual realm, if we fail to close doors, the accuser can access our minds and torment us. If you simply cut someone off without verbally expressing your offense or making it clear that the relationship has ended, you risk remaining in a mental and spiritual prison from within.

As you read this, certain faces may come to mind—people with whom situations didn't end well. If you have a way to reach them, consider taking steps to bring closure. This will effectively prevent the enemy from using unresolved issues to gain access to your heart. Shame, guilt, and unforgiveness will no longer **grant the enemy legal access** to your peace of mind. God does not intend for His children to experience partial healing or endure a life of bondage. The Word of God says, Whom the Son sets free is truly free indeed.

Wisdom Principle: The approach to closing doors may vary depending on the situation and individuals involved. Seek wise counsel from trusted authority figures, such as a minister or pastor.

For instance, shutting the door on an abusive relationship may require legal intervention, while handling a disrespectful child who lives under your supervision demands a different approach. A parent who recently found Christ cannot expect their teenager— who witnessed them living contrary to God's ways—to suddenly embrace a new faith journey. **Forced spiritual environments can backfire.** As the head of the household, you have authority, but God calls parents to train their children in the way they should go with love and honor.

Raising children requires the Lord's help. Every parent faces unique struggles based on their child needs. **Relationships often expose our weaknesses and force personal growth.** It is painful yet necessary to allow prayer and fasting to refine our hearts in difficult situations.

Understanding the root of your pain gives you an advantage over both your flesh and the enemy. Now is the time to shut the door completely, armed with the knowledge and power of the Holy Spirit. Be patient with yourself, track your growth, and seek wise counsel when needed. You are a warrior in God's kingdom—do not fight alone.

Key Takeaways:

1. Come into agreement with your new season—determine who can go with you.
2. When there is unresolved offense, the window remains open.
3. Satan gains legal access if we do not address spiritual matters properly.
4. You cannot force anyone into a relationship with God, including your children.

Chapter Five

Peer Pressure

Principle Scripture:

"Whoever acknowledges me before others, I will also acknowledge before my Father in heaven. But whoever disowns me before others, I will disown before my Father in heaven." — Matthew 10:32-33 (NIV)

This chapter requires your participation. The Word of God is a lamp unto your feet and a comfort when you feel alone. You can do all things through Christ Jesus, who strengthens you.

The Intimidation of Fear

Peer pressure is a common struggle during childhood and adolescence. However, spiritual peer pressure also exists, though it is not often discussed. This type of pressure arises when we must make public or private decisions that align with our faith.

In Matthew 26:69-75, when Jesus was being persecuted, the very disciples who once walked with Him denied Him. They buckled under pressure, fearing the consequences of association with Jesus. Today, believers face similar challenges. Following Christ often means abandoning worldly pursuits—changing friendships, habits, and influences. Even small decisions, such as the music we listen to, can impact our spiritual walk.

Music, while created by God, can be weaponized by the enemy to subtly influence our thoughts and emotions. It can resurface old desires, leading us back to past behaviors. Peer pressure often comes through the people and things we love the most.

Peer pressure can also stem from family traditions or cultural norms. In some households, coercing people into compliance is normalized. Many believers assume that because they are saved, those around them will naturally align. However, peer pressure can even manifest within Christian circles—sometimes in the form of joking or guilt-tripping.

In Matthew 10, Jesus warns that if we disown Him before others, He will disown us before the Father. While we may not intentionally reject God, we often do so in subtle ways—compromising our values to avoid conflict or staying silent when we witness wrongdoing. Workplace and church environments are prime places where this occurs. God observes our integrity in both public and private settings.

Luke 22:54-64 recounts how Jesus' disciples abandoned Him under pressure. Fear and intimidation led them to deny their association with Him. Fear does not come from God. If a request or expectation causes fear or anxiety, it is likely not from Him.

As followers of Christ, we must accept everything that comes with our faith, including rejection and misunderstanding.

Stay your course, warrior. The Word of God will refine you, and in due season, heaven will publicly declare who you belong to. When we stand firm in faith, God grants power and authority over the enemy. As members of His kingdom, we are under divine protection. Fear not!

Now Let's See What We Learned:
1. Define peer pressure vs. spiritual peer pressure.
2. How you treat people reflects how you honor God.
3. Daily life choices can unintentionally display dishonor toward God.
4. Denying God in public mirrors your personal relationship with Him.

I pray that this book becomes a go-to manual—second only to the Bible—as you embark on this new journey of prayer and fasting unto the Lord.

Encouragement Scripture

2 Timothy 1:6-7 (Berean Standard Bible)

"For this reason, I remind you to fan into flame the gift of God, which is in you through the laying on of my hands. For God has not given us a spirit of fear, but of power, love, and self-control."

A Moment of Transparency

Prayer has become my daily weapon in spiritual warfare against the devil. Through years of suffering, trials, and tribulations, I've learned valuable lessons—though, at times, I've repeated tests. I think we all struggle with working alongside others and loving unconditionally. We should love others, not merely tolerate them, as we sometimes do with coworkers and family members. If you need a reason to learn how to pray, here's a big one: "To love one another."

Prayer is a powerful weapon, but love keeps you fully equipped. With the love of Christ, you will never run out of ammunition.

Some may wonder, "Where do the bullets come from, and what does that have to do with prayer?" Sometimes, developing an imagination helps us understand how to fight effectively in the spirit. If you continue reading, you'll see that my imagination comes from the west side of Dayton, Ohio— 'the hood' – laugh out loud.

If you understand how a gun functions in the real world, then visualizing prayer as a spiritual weapon can enhance your effectiveness and confidence in the Holy Ghost. Have you ever seen someone in a movie with a fully loaded gun compared to someone with an empty chamber? The latter may start off with a loud bark, but eventually, they retreat because they aren't truly prepared.

Many believers enter prayer confidently after hearing a Sunday message, ready to fight and out of nowhere, the devil delivers a crushing blow, attacking the mind or body, leaving us questioning the effectiveness of our prayers. We ask, "Where is God in this?"

Many spiritual battles arise from dealing with people. They will test your patience to the point where you forget you're not fighting against flesh and blood. It happens to the best of us.

Learning to pray can be challenging. People often say, "Prayer is a lifestyle," and that's true. Others say, "Prayer is simply communication with God," which is also accurate. I don't believe most believers struggle with praying—I believe they struggle with understanding how to use prayer as a weapon, a tool, an instrument, and a direct line of communication with God, rather than merely performing religious rituals.

Yes, many people are worshiping prayer. Sometimes, without realizing it, we desire to appear spiritually strong so badly that we focus more on the sound of prayer rather than the lifestyle of prayer—holy and acceptable. We rehearse it, memorize scriptures, and perform outwardly, but true power comes from understanding the righteousness that avails much.

We don't struggle with prayer itself; we struggle with righteous living. If Prayer is simply a conversation with God, so why do we find it difficult to speak with Him daily?

I believe people would pray more if they understood how to apply the Word to their lives practically. Prayer becomes easier when practiced daily. How? Because every day, we have something to talk about. Remember, prayer is communication, but its effectiveness lies in righteousness. I'm going to show you how to use prayer as your weapon.

It's all about understanding. The Bible says in Proverbs 4:7, "Above all these things, get understanding." I believe you picked up this book because you have unanswered questions and seek practical understanding. Maybe you're asking one of the following questions:

1. "Why is prayer difficult for me?"
2. "Why do I struggle with consistency?"
3. "Why do I feel like I'm not praying correctly?"

Perhaps it's insecurity about the righteousness of your lifestyle. So, let's break things down, chapter by chapter, and overcome these hindrances together!

Perception is everything. The more we seek the characteristics of God, the clearer our knowledge and understanding of His righteousness become. Your faith will increase as you live out the Word. As John 1:1-4 states, "In the beginning was the Word, and the Word was with God, and the Word was God. And the Word became flesh and dwelt among us."

Let's get to work! It's time to fight back and take control of your mind through prayer.

Now let's answer these questions:

1. Define peer pressure vs. spiritual peer pressure.
2. Do you believe how you treat people, reflects how you honor God?
3. Daily life choices can unintentionally display dishonor toward God? Yes or No? Explain your answer.
4. Denying God in public mirrors your personal relationship with Him. Yes or No? Explain your answer.

Chapter Six

I'm Married but I Feel Single

Principle Scriptures

James 4:7 – *"Submit yourselves, then, to God. Resist the devil, and he will flee from you."*

Romans 12:1 – *"Therefore, I urge you, brothers and sisters, in view of God's mercy, to offer your bodies as a living sacrifice, holy and pleasing to God—this is your true and proper worship."*

The Three-Strand Cord

Ecclesiastes 4:12 states, "A cord of three strands is not easily broken." As long as Christ remains the center of the marriage, the Lord will back everything connected to Him. You, your spouse, and Christ form a three-strand cord. Be encouraged and stand strong in the Lord. Marriage is hard work, but your labor in prayer, forgiveness, and love will reap an expected harvest in due season.

The battle within marriage often arises when it seems like the devil is using your spouse to bring division into the home. Can I get an amen?

Marriage is a covenant formed at the altar, but it later requires both individuals to look inward through the altar unto God. Self-examination is crucial—identifying open access points the devil might exploit. Many married couples I have counseled, they often say, they gained so much wisdom and insight they've learned about themselves through marriage, often wishing they had started their inner healing journey while still single.

Seeking healing—whether through therapy, pastoral guidance, healing is vital. Certain strongholds require the anointing of God to break yokes, especially those rooted in childhood trauma. The devil manipulates unresolved wounds, using them as weapons against us. In response, we learn to build walls around our hearts, determined never to experience similar pain again.

When you're married but still feel single, it may indicate that past wounds are standing in the way of the new covenant. These barriers need to be acknowledged and destroyed.

Often in marriage, conflict arises when two believers turn against each other rather than recognizing the true enemy—the devil. He is the invisible adversary who sows discord and then hides, convincing each spouse to blame the other.

In any covenant, two spirits become one. When division enters, you are essentially fighting against yourself. The Bible warns, "A kingdom divided cannot stand." To strengthen your marriage, spiritual warfare must be recognized and addressed through prayer, healing, and unity.

Let's uncover the root causes

Break the chains, and reclaim the peace that God intended for your marriage!

Let's dig a little deeper. If you are in a covenant relationship with someone and, despite your efforts to seek counsel or resolve issues, the other party refuses to make any effort, you may need to step back until emotions settle. Then, begin fighting for the marriage in the spirit. This strategy only works if you put aside pride and focus on submitting to God. The Lord will guide and teach you how to demonstrate His love through suffering. Have you seen the movie "War Room" by Kendrick Brothers Production? it's a must see how you can war for your marriage without fighting against the person.

Forgiveness and the Foundation of Marriage

While there are numerous biblical strategies to preserve a marriage, it will always begin with forgiveness and a willingness to release grudges. However, the relationship will not last if the foundation is not built on the principles of God, as God is love. The enemy often creates confusion and division within covenants, making it easier to attack a union when there is offense or lack of loyalty. Understanding that marriage is the union of two individuals who must become one is a process that takes time. The enemy preys on childhood weaknesses, reopening old wounds, which can lead to blame-shifting, just as Eve did in the garden of Eden in the book of Genesis in the bible.

Spiritual Warfare in Marriage

When the enemy infiltrates a marriage through sin, such as adultery or unforgiveness, he seeks to claim the wages of that sin. Unforgiveness acts as an open door for spiritual torment. Since we wrestle not against flesh and blood but against principalities (Ephesians 6:12), the enemy legally attacks marriages through bitterness, offense, and division. This torment can affect all aspects of life, including children, finances, and ministry. However, God has given us every spiritual weapon needed to overcome the flesh and gain victory over the enemy.

Even when a spouse refuses to communicate or act righteously, **the pressure you feel can be transformed into intercession**. Praying for your spouse will increase your capacity for love. **The fruit of love is the most powerful weapon in spiritual battles**. Applying these principles requires time, intentional effort, wisdom from God, and sometimes, wise counsel. Ultimately, it demands the willingness to become a living sacrifice, laying down pride.

The Power of Consistency in Prayer

Consistent prayer dismantles offense because it is difficult to hate those you continually pray for. When married, but feeling spiritually single due to disagreements or financial conflicts, your prayer room must become both your place of comfort and battleground for war—just like in the movie War Room. Submitting to God and the Holy Spirit daily will provide guidance. Learning to love through Christ's lens after an offense is crucial for maintaining the covenant.

Be encouraged, intercessor: God heals and delivers simultaneously. Those with a quick temper or sharp tongue will often go through a season of heart refinement, as the words we speak can destroy our spouse. Both men and women may struggle with using hurtful words, using them to prove a point rather than heal.

Spiritual Growth and Overcoming Attacks

Character development and spiritual fruit are not produced overnight. When we begin to do good, God prunes us further (John 15:2). God is sovereign and can use any situation to bring His word to pass, even conflict in marriage. When under constant attack, it is vital to return to God's Word and examine our own hearts. Without Christ backing us, we stand no chance against the enemy and his dark forces. No matter what your marriage looks like, God cares for His people and hears the cries of His children. The battle belongs to the Lord, but our alignment with God matters.

If our hearts are not in right standing, even though God is just, He cannot go against His Word simply because we are uncomfortable or distressed. However, He uses pain to redirect us back to Him. Sometimes, the fire is your spouse or the ones you love most, but God cares about you both.

God's Power to Restore

In the Bible, it states that the more Pharaoh afflicted the Israelites, the more they grew (Exodus 1:12). This does not mean God always teaches through pain, but rather, He allows trials to strengthen and refine us. He is the Lord of Hosts and the King of Kings, yet also our loving Father and Creator. He has the power to reshape the broken into something new, purely out of His love.

Sometimes, God will send strangers or prophetic dreams to warn and guide you. He is never surprised by the enemy's schemes. **Trust the process of suffering that leads to obedience and submission to the Lord.**

A Season of Pruning and Healing

The Holy Spirit will hold your hand through the daily pruning process. Pain is not your enemy; it is the fertilizer for spiritual growth (Galatians 5:22-23). The more you yield to God, the more He will heal your marriage.

Keep going, warrior—keep going.

Chapter Seven

Hindered Prayers

Key Scriptures:

Matthew 5:24 (KJV): "Leave there thy gift before the altar, and go thy way; first be reconciled to thy brother, and then come and offer thy gift."

Matthew 6:14-15 (NIV): "For if you forgive other people when they sin against you, your heavenly Father will also forgive you. But if you do not forgive others their sins, your Father will not forgive your sins."

Matthew 5:25 highlights the importance of reconciling with our brothers, as unresolved issues not only create division but also hold us accountable to a standard of integrity. Unity in the body of Christ is essential, and God will reject an offering given by someone harboring unforgiveness. His kingdom operates on faith and love—two essential elements that make the prayers of the righteous effective.

Let's get straight to the point: often a lot of today hindered prayers come through offense. Offense will trap you in a mental and spiritual prison. The enemy will use people to hurt you, then hide his hand, using your response to the pain as an access point to attack your mind, body, and soul. The devil does not play fair; he seeks to steal, kill, and destroy (John 10:10). Since he cannot kill without permission, he aims to destroy from within by planting seeds of offense.

Many avoid discussing offense to prevent anger, but ignoring the issue does not heal it. If someone lies, steals, or abuses us, we must acknowledge it and handle it biblically.

Offense in the Church

Imagine a minor conflict between two church ushers. Rather than resolving it, they ignore each other but continue serving. Weeks pass, and division spreads throughout the church. The enemy uses offense to bring discord and division (Song of Solomon 2:15).

If we fail to address issues, the enemy can accuse us in the courts of heaven (Matthew 5:25). Forgiveness is for both parties, not just the one who was hurt. Avoiding someone is a sign that unresolved bitterness remains.

Communication Over Confrontation

Communication is not confrontation—it can be the beginning of a true relationship. Hurtful situations can make receiving correction difficult. The Word of God alone is also defensive, but the Holy Spirit teaches us God's ways if we yield to Him daily. A divided kingdom cannot stand (Mark 3:25). No two people can walk together unless they agree—including you and God, or you and others.

The Danger of Unforgiveness

Unforgiveness hinders your personal relationship with God period. It is wise to seek peaceful closure, even if both parties agree to disagree.

Offense often times can work for you verse against you. Having difficult conversations **in Love** will water the seeds that are planted within. Though pain can create false perceptions, unresolved offense will eventually reshape your perspective on life and God.

God is leading you into a season of deliverance, renewal, and spiritual growth. Keep moving forward, warrior—your breakthrough is near. Stand firm in faith, forgive, and fight the good fight of faith!

Many times, we desire growth, but we may not be prepared for the process that occurs under pressure or the unexpected loss of a loved one. Even when people wrong you, you can still gain in the end if you learn how to use prayer and the power of the Holy Ghost. He will teach you how to respond to the hurt rather than avoid it. Trust me, simply moving away from people does not settle the issue that lies deep in your heart and soul. The "out of sight, out of mind" concept can only hide pain and suffering for so long before the seed of offense begins to bear fruit in one's character, potentially altering how you perceive others who resemble those from your past.

The Power of Pain and Offense

Pain has a way of creating a false reality based on feelings rather than facts. Trauma, in many ways, can blind one to the truth. If you allow hurt or offense to remain unresolved in your heart, it will eventually surface and reshape your perspective on life and even your view of God. Just know you are not alone. God is leading you on a new journey, called life after death—just like Jesus on the cross. This is the beginning of deliverance, even now, as you read this book.

Key Takeaways:

1. Acknowledging the offense gives you an advantage over Satan.

2. Your response can change the outcome of the seed sown in your heart.

3. Unresolved offense will hinder your personal relationship with God and others.

4. Offense affects everyone around you.

Chapter Eight

Waiting on God or Do I Move Forward?

Key Scriptures

"Then God said, 'Let us make mankind in our image, in our likeness, so that they may rule over the fish in the sea, the birds in the sky, the livestock, and all the wild animals, and over all the creatures that move along the ground.'" —Genesis 1:26 (NIV)

"But seek ye first the kingdom of God, and His righteousness, and all these things shall be added unto you." —Matthew 6:33 (KJV)

The Challenge of Waiting

Waiting can be incredibly frustrating, especially when the situation feels urgent. Speaking from experience, it is even more difficult to wait on a God you barely know. Every child of God must go through seasons of waiting to truly understand what they seek. Many times, when we pray for something, it may not come to pass if it is not aligned with His will for our lives. Over time, our prayers evolve, and we begin to sing songs like "I Give Myself Away" by William McDowell and "All I Want Is for You to Be Glorified" by Maranda Curtis giving indication that flesh is dying to self "lol."

When God does not respond immediately or in the way we expect, our hearts are revealed. There is nothing easy about waiting, but seeking God in the process will deliver you from things you didn't even realize needed healing. One example is doubt—waiting will quickly expose whether you truly believe in the God you serve. Doubt will Definitely hinder prayers, James 1:7-8 warns, "For that man ought not to expect to receive anything from the Lord, being a double-minded man, unstable in all his ways."

Understanding Your Role

When you commit to seeking God first and His righteousness, you will experience personal encounters that strengthen your faith. A clear understanding of your position in the kingdom, His righteousness, and His nature can provide strength during times of uncertainty. Many people either grow up in church with only religious knowledge or come to faith later, seeking a personal encounter with God. Regardless of your background, building a personal relationship with Him daily is essential.

Many believers over-spiritualize waiting on God, using it as an excuse to delay action. However, one of the first lessons God teaches is how to partner with Him. Since God is a spirit, He requires vessels on earth to accomplish His will. If you do not understand your role as a child of God, you may find yourself perpetually waiting rather than taking action.

Jesus declared on the cross, "It is finished." This means our participation with heaven is necessary to bring God's kingdom to earth. The Holy Spirit, our Comforter and Guide, empowers believers to act in alignment with God's will. Prayer is a powerful spiritual weapon, but faith must be paired with works to see results. Many religious habits, such as saying, "I need to fast to hear from God," or, "I am waiting on direction," can sometimes become forms of bondage if they prevent believers from taking action.

Learning When to Act

Fasting and prayer are essential disciplines, but we must recognize that many of God's promises are already given. They manifest when we walk in obedience and alignment with His Word. Without understanding our role, waiting on God can lead to frustration, anger, or even hopelessness. Be encouraged—God may be preparing you for His promise, or what you are asking for has an appointed time to manifest.

Waiting on God refines and strengthens faith, just as it did for Abraham and Sarah. Genesis 18:12-15 shows how their barrenness had a divine purpose—to birth a nation. Though God made Abraham a promise, he still had to act in faith and try again physically with Sarah. Similarly, even when we know God's promises, if we do not take action, we may feel as though His Word is not coming to pass.

The Balance Between Waiting and Acting

Waiting should not replace obedience. Many believers struggle with understanding when to move forward. They seek God's instructions but fail to recognize when He is silent, His answer may be within that silence. God has already revealed many things in His Word, yet some delay action under the guise of waiting for further instruction. This hesitation can lead to indirect disobedience. Waiting too long or acting prematurely both have consequences. Those who had to wait on God in the Bible—such as kings, prophets, and leaders—were already established in their faith. We, too, must develop our relationship with God to discern His voice clearly.

It is essential to:

- Seek God's kingdom and righteousness first (Matthew 6:33).
- Recognize the biblical examples of waiting and participation.
- Identify whether God requires action or patience in your situation.

Moving Forward with Faith

A practical way to break free from learned religious behaviors is by identifying biblical principles that resonate with your circumstances. Seeking wise counsel and understanding scriptural requirements for participation can help bring clarity. **Once you have fulfilled spiritual and natural responsibilities, you can confidently declare that you are waiting on God's appointed time.**

Final Encouragement

Whatever you are praying and believing for must first be established in the spiritual realm by faith. Start with prayer, declare God's Word over it, and seek wise counsel. God will surround you with people who can testify to His faithfulness. His Word will speak directly to you as you seek Him by faith. Preparation is key—your prayer life, obedience, and consistency behind closed doors will determine the outcome.

The Bible repeatedly shows that God instructs His people to move forward—whether by a guiding cloud in Exodus 13:21 or providing daily manna in Exodus 16. God sustains those who actively participate in their faith.

Let's Pray! Read this out loud.

Heavenly Father, you know exactly what I need. There are things I have been praying and waiting for, and I seek clarity on when to act. As I wait, renew my strength, create in me a clean heart, and renew the right spirit within me. I commit to working out my salvation, walking in obedience, and seeking Your kingdom first. Teach me Your ways and give me a hunger for Your Word. In Jesus' name, Amen.

I thank You in advance, Lord, for what You are doing in me and around me, in Jesus' name. Teach me how to wait patiently in You, God, with joy. Deliver me completely from all frustration, anger, and fear of the unknown that leads me to make rash decisions instead of waiting on You. Forgive me for doubting what You have said in Your word concerning my life during my hard seasons. Lord, give me the Holy Ghost boldness, like the Lion of Judah, to go after the promises of God that You have already said that has been given to me. Fill me with Your wisdom, Lord, and Your peace as I keep my mind on You. In Jesus' name, Amen..

Chapter Nine

Living with the Inner Enemy

Principle Scripture

Romans 7:14-15

"We know that the Law is spiritual, but I am a creature of the flesh [worldly, self-reliant—carnal and unspiritual], sold into slavery to sin [and serving under its control]. For I do not understand my own actions [I am baffled and bewildered by them]. I do not practice what I want to do, but I am doing the very thing I hate [and yielding to my human nature, my worldliness—my sinful capacity]."

The Battle Within

Have you ever wanted to change, but it seemed impossible because of your current situation or an addiction to certain habits that bring temporary ease to the mind? Over time, we learn to enjoy painful pleasures that come with lifelong consequences. Often, we engage in behaviors we know are unhealthy, yet determined to live for the moment. Like settling for toxic relationships and returning to some old habits that may seem like an escape, but ultimately lead to depression and even suicidal thoughts.

The war within is a different kind of fight—one that only the power of the Holy Ghost can help us overcome. The battle against ourselves is real, revealing that our flesh and emotions can be greater adversaries than even Satan's direct attacks. Understanding more about our sinful nature, beginning in Genesis, brings deeper clarity on how to war from within.

Overcoming Condemnation

Do not be so hard on yourself. Do not allow your mistakes to keep you trapped in guilt and shame. Instead, strive daily to yield to the Holy Ghost. Repent and turn from your wicked ways, allowing God to heal you with His love. Even when it feels like nothing is changing and you are failing to live righteously, do not grow weary in well-doing; the Lord will uphold you.

Going to church alone does not always equip us for the mental and spiritual challenges that arise from trauma or abuse. Under God's lens, weakness is not a flaw but an opportunity for His power to flow abundantly (Romans 8:26). Without Him, we can do nothing in our strength. When we acknowledge our limitations, pride is exposed, and our focus shifts toward Jesus Christ, who has overcome all things without sin.

Healing Through God and Support

Religious activities alone do not always bring deliverance from internal strongholds. I strongly believe in seeking both Jesus and professional counseling, such as therapy or pastoral guidance, for inner healing.

The areas where you feel most vulnerable are the very places you must surrender to God daily for divine healing. Ignoring pain or unresolved trauma stunts spiritual growth and gives the enemy room to manipulate weaknesses. When we neglect to seek counsel or deliverance, confusion and fear infiltrate our minds. Instead of having power over fear, we adjust our lives to avoid anything that makes us uncomfortable.

As Matthew 12:45 warns, when one spirit enters, seven more may follow. This is how confusion, doubt, and unbelief take root in a believer's heart, often without realization—until the right wrong button is pushed.

Recognizing and Addressing Inner Wounds

Dealing with childhood trauma that manifests as adult struggles can be challenging. Often, we do not realize how damaged our souls are until we enter marriage, parenthood, or ministry. Not all inner wounds are immediately detectable, which is why we must rely on God and the Holy Spirit for daily guidance and healing.

Our emotions can be deceptive. When we say, "I feel led to do something," we must ask ourselves: Is this the flesh, a past wound, or the Spirit of God leading me?

The best advice I can offer is to lay all your weaknesses at the altar and daily acknowledge your need for the Holy Spirit's guidance. When you release your burdens, God exchanges them for His lighter yoke. Stay committed to this healing journey; every season has an end.

Not only will God wash you white as snow, but He will also use what once tried to destroy you to rebuild you from the inside out.

Key Takeaways:

1. Pleasure does not change reality.
2. The war against yourself is real.
3. Unresolved issues create space for spiritual attacks.

Chapter Ten

The Benefits of Waiting Patiently

Principle Scripture

"I waited patiently for the Lord; and he inclined unto me, and heard my cry. He brought me up also out of a horrible pit, out of the miry clay, and set my feet upon a rock, and established my goings." —Psalms 40:1-2 (KJV)

The Challenge of Waiting

Waiting is not always easy. You may not be physically doing anything, yet waiting often leads to frustration, especially when it comes to things like food service or doctor's appointments. However, if we trust that the outcome is worth the wait, we endure.

Similarly, in our spiritual lives, many factors contribute to delays, even when we know God's promises have been secured through Jesus' blood.

What to Do While Waiting

During your season of waiting, worship the Lord, seek His guidance, and immerse yourself in His Word. Waiting patiently transforms your faith and aligns you with God's will. Psalm 84:11 reminds us that God withholds no good thing from those who walk uprightly.

If you have been praying for years without seeing results, it is easy to grow discouraged. Often, we only hear half of God's promises preached, missing the instructions attached to them. Waiting is part of the salvation journey, shaping our faith beyond the constraints of time.

God's Response to Waiting

Psalm 40:1-4 reveals that David's patience led God to incline His ear toward him. Notice that David did not address God as King or Almighty but as Lord—signifying God's readiness to intervene with power and authority.

When we maintain faith during waiting, we experience:

- Deliverance from pits of despair.
- A firm foundation under our feet.
- An established path forward.
- A renewed song of praise.

Encouragement in Waiting

Study God's character so you know what to expect when waiting on His promises. Just as you trust a reputable doctor or restaurant, trust that the Lord—who has proven Himself before—will not fail you now. Keep waiting patiently until breakthrough comes, whether in your situation or within you.

Scriptural Encouragement:

James 1:2-4 — "Count it all joy when ye fall into diver's temptations; knowing this, that the trying of your faith worketh patience. But let patience have her perfect work, that ye may be perfect and entire, wanting nothing."

Chapter Eleven

Misplaced Love/The Seed of Rejection

Principle Scripture

"But the Lord inflicted serious diseases on Pharaoh and his household because of Abram's wife Sarai. So Pharaoh summoned Abram. 'What have you done to me?' he said. 'Why didn't you tell me she was your wife?'" —Genesis 12:17-18

Understanding Love: Worldly vs. Godly Love

Let's explore the difference between what the world defines as love and what God calls love.

Worldly love is often based solely on emotions, media portrayals, or materialistic gestures. Many times, movies and popular culture equate love with physical attraction and transactional relationships. Some view love through the lens of what can be given or received, defining its worth through material possessions. However, biblical love is quite different.

From a scriptural standpoint, love should bear the fruits mentioned in Galatians 5:22-23: love, joy, peace, patience, kindness, goodness, faithfulness, gentleness, and self-control. Additionally, love is reflected in how we treat others as an act of worship unto God.

1 John 4:8 states, "He who does not love does not know God, for God is love." This means that when we claim to love someone, it is a direct reflection of our love for God. The deeper our relationship with God, the more we learn to love ourselves and, in turn, extend genuine love to others. Mark 12:31 establishes this order of love: seek God first, learn to love yourself as Christ loves you, and then love your neighbor as yourself. *Often, people grow up loving others before loving themselves,* leading to emotional devastation when relationships fail. This is because true love is not rooted in placing others above ourselves but in understanding love through God's perspective.

When love is misplaced—when we love others more than ourselves—it may stem from brokenness or the lust of the flesh rather than genuine, godly love.

The Influence of Early Experiences on Love

Understanding love begins in the home. Whether love was modeled positively in childhood or learned later through encounters with God and family, our early experiences shape our perception of love. Many parents express love by providing for physical needs—paying bills and ensuring food is on the table—without necessarily demonstrating affection. A toxic or traumatic childhood can distort our understanding of love, causing us to seek validation in unhealthy ways. This can lead to skepticism when receiving kindness, questioning others' motives instead of embracing love freely.

However, God's love is different. He loves us unconditionally, without expecting anything in return. That's what makes Him a good Father. Loving oneself can be challenging, especially when struggling with low self-esteem. Yet, God sent His Son, Jesus, to redeem us, and through Him, we learn the true essence of love. The moment we surrender to God, the Holy Spirit works within us to transform our hearts and renew our minds. Prioritizing God helps us set healthy boundaries in relationships and love others appropriately.

Key Takeaways:

1. Define the difference between worldly love and God's love.
2. Every household demonstrates love differently.
3. Misplaced love can negatively impact those around you.
4. Keeping God first aligns all other relationships.

Chapter Twelve

I Need Help but I Don't Want Help

Principle Scriptures:

- *2 Kings 5:12-13 – Naaman initially rejected the prophet's instructions for healing due to pride.*
- *Mark 6:5 – Jesus could do few miracles due to people's unbelief.*

Many people struggle with receiving help but, yet resisting it. Sometimes, it's not about admitting we need help but rather dealing with past disappointments when others have failed us. Have you ever asked for help, only to be let down? Over time, experiences like these can lead us to believe that seeking help is futile, resulting in a self-reliant mindset.

Pride can manifest in various ways. It can appear as arrogance, but it can also take the form of refusing help out of fear of vulnerability. When we avoid seeking assistance, we might be unknowingly harboring hidden pride, rooted in past wounds. The heart is deceitful (Jeremiah 17:9), and pride can disguise itself as independence when, in reality, it may stem from unhealed trauma.

The Role of Communication in Receiving Help

People define and perceive help differently. Like not understanding what some words mean or the person intentions when texting. Miscommunication can create rifts in relationships, particularly when words are misinterpreted. ***Offense often leads to avoidance***, as unresolved rejection wounds make conversations feel like confrontations. Developing strong communication skills helps prevent misunderstandings and fosters healing within the body of Christ.

The Bible teaches us that God desires for us to ask, seek, and knock (Matthew 7:7). Asking breaks down pride, making room for humility. In 2 Kings 5, Naaman almost missed his healing because he wanted it on his terms. Similarly, we sometimes reject God's methods for helping us because they don't align with our expectations.

Pride and Receiving Help

God often sends help in unexpected ways, sometimes through people we least expect. *There are times when God allows us to go without human help so that we can rely solely on Him.* Yet, He also brings the right people into our lives when we are ready to receive guidance.

Unaddressed past wounds—such as fatherlessness, childhood trauma, or spiritual abuse—can impact how we seek and receive help. The discomfort of receiving help can make us reject it, perceiving assistance as control rather than support. Nonetheless, even Jesus needed others to fulfill His purpose on the cross.

> **Key Takeaways:**
> 1. Unhealed wounds can hinder relationships and communication.
> 2. Avoiding help can be rooted in pride.
> 3. The heart is deceitful; always check the source of your feelings.
> 4. Help often comes in ways we don't expect and requires obedience.

Encouragement and Prayer

Your life is a prophecy, and God will watch over you until His word is fulfilled. This book serves as a manual and a prophetic sign that 'you will live and not die' during life's transitions. You are stepping into a new season of blessings and favor.

Let's Pray! Read this out loud.

Dear Father, in the name of Jesus, I surrender my life to You completely. I repent of all my sins, including pride, fear, and unforgiveness. I renounce all strongholds and demonic covenants that have kept me bound through my old habits and ways In Jesus' name Amen, I command every tormenting spirit in my mind and body to leave me now. Father, I thank You for ordering my steps and teaching me to follow Your ways. I declare that whom the Son sets free is free indeed!

AND I AM FREE!

Chapter Thirteen

Encouraging Words

A Call to Action

For those seeking deeper understanding, I invite you to join a prophetic prayer training class. My assignment is to equip upcoming leaders and Leaders of the fivefold ministry, training others how to live a lifestyle of prayer and spiritual warfare. Over the next few years, I will conduct in-person and Zoom training sessions to impart wisdom and spiritual tools for maintaining breakthroughs. Hunger for righteousness must be met with knowledge and action. Email us today @Pbipministry@yahoo.com message us today for details on next Impartation Training classes. Please give 48-72hrs to respond to all emails I will personally respond accordingly.

Thank you

Final Thought

Remember Warrior this is not just a book—it is a life manual. Carry it with you, apply it's lessons throughout life, and walk boldly in your God-given authority.

I am praying and rooting for you, don't give up in transition.

Final Prayer:

May the Lord grant you strength and wisdom to apply the lessons from this book. Everything He has for you is yours to receive. In Jesus' name, may you walk in wholeness and divine purpose. Amen.

God bless you,

I love you on purpose

Made in the USA
Coppell, TX
29 September 2025

60665548R00046